D0773396

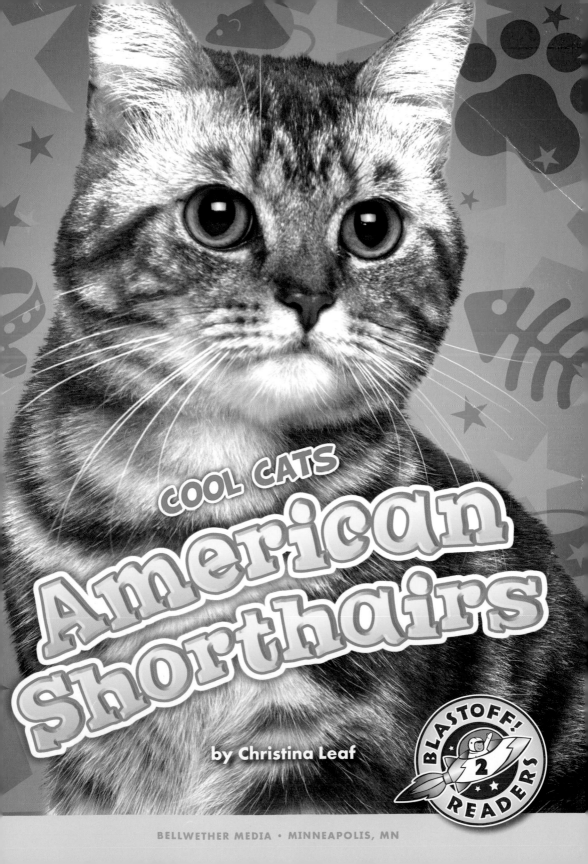

COOL CATS

American Shorthairs

by Christina Leaf

BLASTOFF!
2
READERS

BELLWETHER MEDIA · MINNEAPOLIS, MN

Note to Librarians, Teachers, and Parents:

Blastoff! Readers are carefully developed by literacy experts and combine standards-based content with developmentally appropriate text.

Level 1 provides the most support through repetition of high-frequency words, light text, predictable sentence patterns, and strong visual support.

Level 2 offers early readers a bit more challenge through varied simple sentences, increased text load, and less repetition of high-frequency words.

Level 3 advances early-fluent readers toward fluency through increased text and concept load, less reliance on visuals, longer sentences, and more literary language.

Level 4 builds reading stamina by providing more text per page, increased use of punctuation, greater variation in sentence patterns, and increasingly challenging vocabulary.

Level 5 encourages children to move from "learning to read" to "reading to learn" by providing even more text, varied writing styles, and less familiar topics.

Whichever book is right for your reader, Blastoff! Readers are the perfect books to build confidence and encourage a love of reading that will last a lifetime!

This edition first published in 2016 by Bellwether Media, Inc.

No part of this publication may be reproduced in whole or in part without written permission of the publisher. For information regarding permission, write to Bellwether Media, Inc., Attention: Permissions Department, 5357 Penn Avenue South, Minneapolis, MN 55419.

Library of Congress Cataloging-in-Publication Data

Leaf, Christina.
   American Shorthairs / by Christina Leaf.
      pages cm. – (Blastoff! Readers. Cool Cats)
   Summary: "Relevant images match informative text in this introduction to American shorthair cats. Intended for students in kindergarten through third grade"– Provided by publisher.
   Audience: Ages 5 to 8
   Audience: K to grade 3
   Includes bibliographical references and index.
   ISBN 978-1-62617-230-2 (hardcover: alk. paper)
   1. American shorthair cat–Juvenile literature. I. Title.
   SF449.A45L43 2016
   636.8–dc23
                        2015007052

Table of Contents

What Are American Shorthairs?	4
History of American Shorthairs	8
A Cat of Many Colors	12
Friendly Yet Independent	16
Glossary	22
To Learn More	23
Index	24

What Are American Shorthairs?

American shorthairs are cats that were **bred** to work.

They were first used to catch **rodents**.

Powerful bodies make them good hunters.

Thick **coats** keep
the short-haired cats
warm outside.

History of American Shorthairs

American shorthairs
were bred in
North America in
the 1600s and 1700s.

England

North
America

N

W E

S

Early **settlers** from England brought cats on ships across the Atlantic Ocean. The cats kept rats out of the food supply.

On land, the cats hunted in barns. They caught rodents that ate crops and animal feed.

Living outside on farms made the cats **hardy**. Over time, the strongest started the American shorthair **breed**.

A Cat of Many Colors

American shorthairs come in more than 80 different coats. They may be one color or patterned.

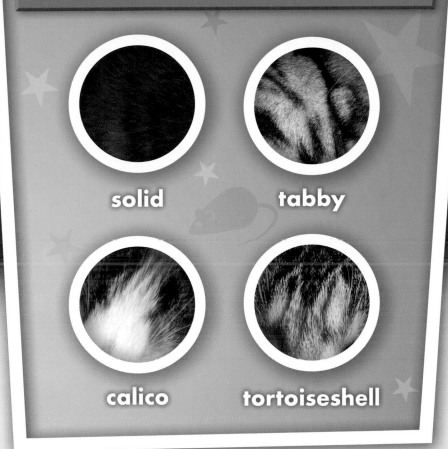

American Shorthair Coats

solid

tabby

calico

tortoiseshell

Tabby is the most common pattern. Others are **calico** and **tortoiseshell**.

American shorthairs are muscular and medium in size. They have wide, round heads and short, pointed ears.

American Shorthair Profile

—— short, pointed ears

—— round, wide head

—— muscular body

Weight: 6 to 15 pounds (3 to 7 kilograms)

Life Span: 15 to 20 years

Friendly Yet Independent

American shorthairs are friendly and easygoing. They like to be with people.

Most get along with other cats
and even dogs.

These **independent** cats do not mind being alone.

Many will play by themselves. They can make anything into a toy.

American shorthairs
use hunting **instincts**
during playtime. They
chase toys and watch
animals outside.

They also love sleeping in the sun!

Glossary

bred—purposely mated two cats to make kittens with certain qualities

breed—a type of cat

calico—a pattern that has patches of white, black, and reddish brown fur

coats—the hair or fur covering some animals

hardy—able to live through difficult conditions

independent—able and willing to do things alone

instincts—ways of behaving or thinking that are not learned

rodents—small animals that gnaw on their food

settlers—people who live in a new place where there are few or no people

tabby—a pattern that has stripes, patches, or swirls of colors

tortoiseshell—a pattern of yellow, orange, and black fur with few or no patches of white

To Learn More

AT THE LIBRARY

Furstinger, Nancy. *American Shorthair Cats.*
Mankato, Minn.: Child's World, 2014.

Holland, Gini. *American Shorthairs.* New York, N.Y.:
PowerKids Press, 2014.

Landau, Elaine. *American Shorthairs Are the Best!*
Minneapolis, Minn.: Lerner Pub. Co., 2011.

ON THE WEB

Learning more about
American shorthairs
is as easy as 1, 2, 3.

1. Go to www.factsurfer.com.

2. Enter "American shorthairs" into the search box.

3. Click the "Surf" button and you will see a
   list of related web sites.

With factsurfer.com, finding more
information is just a click away.

Index

Atlantic Ocean, 9

bodies, 6, 15

bred, 4, 8

breed, 11

catch, 5, 10

chase, 20

coats, 7, 12, 13

color, 12

dogs, 17

ears, 14, 15

England, 8, 9

heads, 14, 15

hunting, 6, 10, 20

independent, 18

instincts, 20

life span, 15

North America, 8

outside, 7, 11, 20

patterns, 12, 13

people, 16

play, 19, 20

rodents, 5, 9, 10

short-haired, 7

size, 14, 15

sleeping, 21

toy, 19, 20

work, 4